The Prophet M Poems, Predictions, & Post
Book 1

Morgan Singletary

RoseDog Books
PITTSBURGH, PENNSYLVANIA 15238

RoseDog Books
585 Alpha Drive, Suite 103
Pittsburgh, PA 15238
Visit our website at www.rosedogbookstore.com

ISBN: 979-8-89027-277-5
eISBN: 979-8-89027-775-6

Forward

My intentions are not to offend anyone with this book. I will be expressing my own personal feelings and if it causes you to explore different perspectives, I have done all that I can do. May God bless you and Christ be with you.

Let's Begin

PEACE

This modern world I'm in seems like no end. Friends turned on me. Friends walked away. It's not for me to say stay. Free will runs about spewing out all types of disgusting things. When the bird sings they want to shut him up, keep him stuck because its not music to their ears, it brings fears and remembered tears so they run away today in this modern world. This modern world, will it ever end?

The Pandemic of 2019

It's time though it seems according to the pandemic 2019 to change some things despite the pain. No NBA this year, fans at the Kentucky Derby hold back your tears. The death toll rise, the look of fear in people eyes. All restaurants closed, bars too. We are currently under a strict curfew. No movements across borders coming from Washington D.C. were the orders.

I sit back and take it all in As I hear about the life passing in sin. Store closed door, store closed door. I'm one of the few outside, I'm careful about my life not scarred to die though.

Gotta do what I gotta do. I got to eat. I don't know about you. So I got my boots on, gloves too, come on pandemic 2019. I ain't scarred of you.

Myth:

Money is the devil's tool.

Busted:

Money is Jesus Christ's tool.

I couldn't think of the words to say to make you understand what I am feeling today. So I ask that you recall times gone by when I was there to see you cry. When you couldn't even dress when we would clean up your mess. Well that role I played my part as best as I could through times I stood. Now its your turn to step into this role.

And since I've gotten old I realized what you needed was not told. I thought what I was teaching was right but the truth was out of my sight. Now the truth has come to view and the truth is what I want to teach you for a better life and bearable strifes. I love you and pass this along. This key factor will make you strong.

Let's talk about this elephant in the room. We all suffer from PTSD now or one time or another. Be kind and patient to your neighbor.

A Whisper

I heard a whisper as I awoke at the onset.
No matter what date is my fate.

Friends

On friends, 98% you can't count on unless you are in the 2% crowd then you can count on 98% of your friends.

I don't know about the boy scouts but let me say what the man scouts do. We get a badge for courage when we see things through a badge for honor of the most high. A badge for love until we die, ribbons for morals are included too.
I don't know about the boy scouts but that's what the man scouts do.

Do all stars explode?

No

only the bad ones.

Is there an alternative medicine?

Yes.

Self-healing but Christ is the only doctor.

W hy didn't you come and tell me when you were at home and turn to stone?

You could have said you were on drugs. I had only love for you. But instead you chose to break my heart for your part. Now its time for me to walk away, but not before I say I love you.

What came first the chicken or the egg?

Duh!
The Egg.
Go Figure.

My Brother

My brother thru the fire I am here
til the smoke clears.
We've been at this war so long,
I know we are both battle torn. Our mission will give us the courage to
fight til we stand tall in the night.
I love you brother. I'm your biggest fan
Now reach out and take my hand.

Heaven's Door

I come to heaven's door straight from hell
full of hatred. All is not well.
It's been a long journey to get to this door.
I had to pick myself up off the floor.
Just had the strength when I thought no more.
Will someone open heaven's door?

Does Heaven Exist?

Yes.

Where is it?

It's in your head.

Will the end of the world come?

Yeah!

When you die otherwise its not.

We are like the sand in an hour glass.

All our sins fall pass.

All the sins we try to hide, take the ride until there's no more.

Does God exist?

Next question.

Is a person born evil or is it society?

Duh, Society.

Let me touch the clouds dance on the moon before life takes me soon.

A glorious life I have nothing to lose.

For the whispers say for my fear choose.

Sounds sweet to me I can be now who.

I want to be worthy free at last free at last.

No boundaries but mind.

They say seek and yee shall find.

It is true, it is true free at last.

Who was at fault in the garden of Eden?

Adam

The Road

One misinformed mason started laying bricks to build his road.
They were the best to
use is what he was told.
As he laid more and look back at his past.
He saw the road built to last has caused everything to crash.

Did man originate from apes?

Well kind of, sort of.
We looked like apes and thought like apes
Otherwise nope!

Are animals dumb?

No.
They are on par with 98% of humans.

What is the soul?

The soul is everything except the heart and Christ.

Does Christimas exist?

Yes.

This one is for the kids and adults.

Teachers

Their jobs will go from hero to zero.

Will computers ever be smarter than man?
No, absolutely not.
Only quicker and thats what counts.

This Land

This land we're in is full of sin but that's not all we have.
If we do things in proper order we can have a laugh.
We can look at people shout, rant and rave.
We can smile inside as we hear lies and see them misbehave.
In this land, our beautiful land we can truly flourish if we
keep our hearts and have our spirits nourished.
We can maintain through the insane.
Let's do it in this land.
Let man begin to know that we can.
That is my hope for this land and my best
wishes goes out to man.

Is there hope?

Yes.

There is hope for everyone but not for all.

Peace.

I thought of cutting you out while in doubt but I came to my senses. To remove you would be a piece missing as I feel before and knew not from the start but to remove you would be removing a piece of my heart.

Should we obey the laws of our government?

Yes.

Should the government obey too?

Yes

Lets look deep inside and what do you see?
Oh no, you abandoned me. It felt so sweet and
wrong but I felt love after long and then I look
around and what do I see?
I see he that abandoned me.

Should we be divided on the fact of getting a shot?

Yes.
But it makes no difference.

We are all divided souls as the story goes
searching for the missing part.
We will not rest or get peace until it's found
by the heart.
The quest for most is all but lost while some
run and hide.
Listen to me and take my hand.
I'll be your guide.

Should we be prejudice?

Yes we should.
But most just cant see the truth.

Why do we split apart listening to the heart?
But the mind knows best and does the rest until
they will be done. In my darkness there is hope
to find what's behind.
Is it you? Is it me? I want to see free.

Does time travel exist?

Yes it does.

Have we made contact with another planet?

Yes we have.

Do we know it?

I'm not sure.

Yes I know.

You are there but here.
It's my love dear.
Do not fear what's around you, just do what
you've been told.
Do not fold.
For if you do this I have told you this truth.
You are there but here.
You are here, not there.
Do not listen to them hear them.
You are there but here till the end, can you un-
derstand?
Because I will keep coming again until you do,
I love you.
You are here, not there.

On Women,

1) Women's life expectancy will decline.

2) Single mothers are about to endure hardship like never seen.

3) Scary increase of women on women violence.

Stand Tall

My eyes are flushed clean.
There goes another dream.
Silence in my ear so loud.
The words of the lip.
The people in the crowd.
The rain, the pain.
It's okay though.
I have felt it before.
Not the first time.
Rain has been at my door in time I know again.
I'll be able to open up the Curtains and let the sun shine in.
When it does I'll step outside.
Stand tall as I pass the people by.

On Laws

With laws I say that the best one that works
for you and the one that will catch you up first is
the law of karma.
It will get you every time.

On Abortion

Women, I understand the surface part covering
choice in this matter.
As well all should consider the surface.
Now I am just one investigator and I see it building
up for women to take greater responsibility for
how they live their life.
Isn't that what you wanted?
Isn't that what you envisioned?
Now prepare yourself ladies.

*I want to dedicate this book to all the suns and moons
that came into my orbit.*

Keep your light shining.